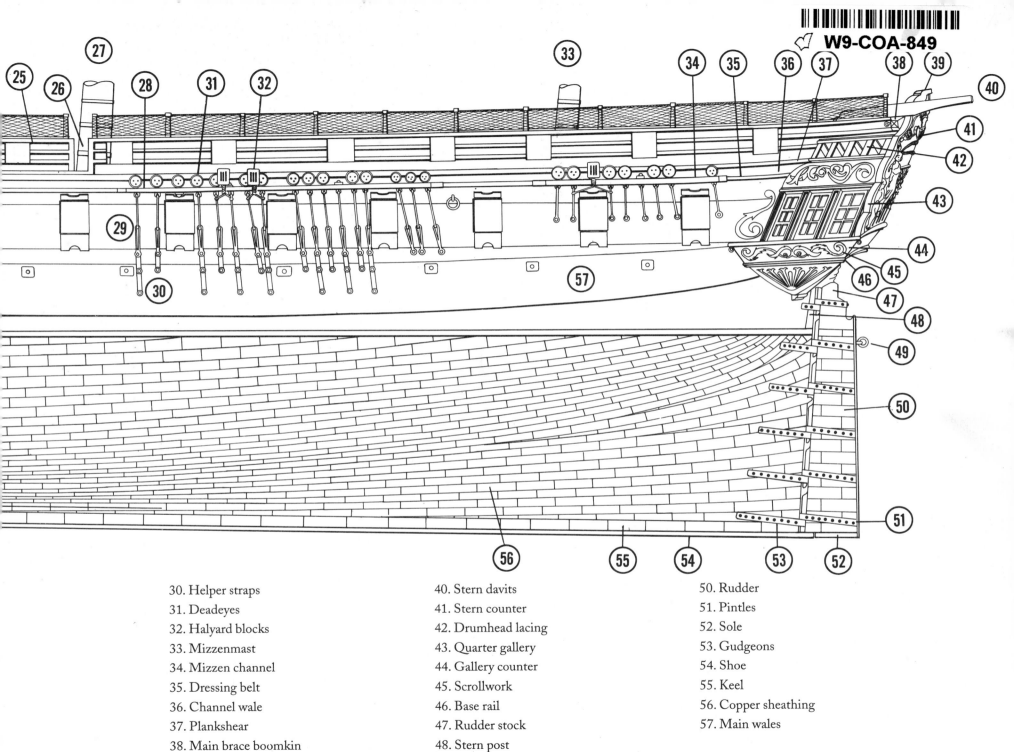

W9-COA-849

30. Helper straps
31. Deadeyes
32. Halyard blocks
33. Mizzenmast
34. Mizzen channel
35. Dressing belt
36. Channel wale
37. Plankshear
38. Main brace boomkin
39. Taffrail

40. Stern davits
41. Stern counter
42. Drumhead lacing
43. Quarter gallery
44. Gallery counter
45. Scrollwork
46. Base rail
47. Rudder stock
48. Stern post
49. Monkey's tail (eye bolt)

50. Rudder
51. Pintles
52. Sole
53. Gudgeons
54. Shoe
55. Keel
56. Copper sheathing
57. Main wales

Old Ironsides

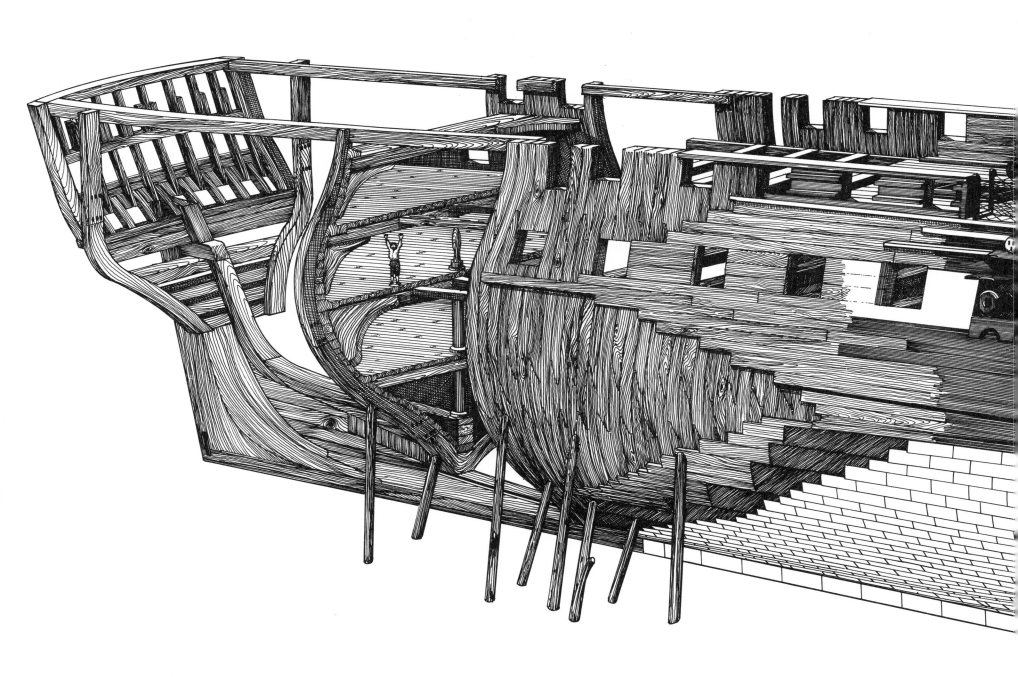

Old Ironsides

Americans Build a Fighting Ship

written and illustrated by

David Weitzman

Houghton Mifflin Company
Boston 1997

For Mariah and Stephen

Prologue

Mr. Washington was angry. The president had just received word of yet another American merchant ship taken by Algerian pirates. The year was 1793, and already eleven American merchantmen had been seized.

This time it was the *Polly*, out of Newburyport, Massachusetts, bound for Cadiz, Spain. The unarmed brig was approached by a ship flying a friendly flag. Only when *Polly* was within cannon range did her captain realize it was actually a pirate ship. The brigands swiftly came up alongside, boarded, and swarmed over the decks and defenseless crew.

The *Polly* was taken as a prize to Algiers. Once there, the crew members were shackled in irons and thrown into filthy dungeons with hundreds of sailors from other nations. Those who did not die from the moldy food or the grueling work of cutting and dragging huge stones fell under the merciless lashings of the slave drivers.

In all, 126 Americans had been captured, and more would surely follow. America had not one man-of-war to protect its growing merchant fleet.

A million dollars! And more! That's what the pirates demanded in ransom and tribute (when Congress had only five million dollars to run the whole country). Before this incident, the president had agreed to pay the humiliating tribute. He would do anything for peace — peace to give his young nation, impoverished and exhausted by the Revolutionary War, time to heal and recover. But there would be no recovery if Americans could not sell their goods in foreign ports.

America needed an armed fleet. Even Thomas Jefferson, long opposed to having any military, agreed that it was now time to "repel force by force." The debates raged in Congress: "The maddest idea in the world," one senator declared; another countered, "No navy, no nation."

Mr. Washington made up his mind. He pleaded for a fleet to protect America "from insult or aggression." And so Congress set aside $688,888.52 — about half the demanded ransom and tribute — to build six American warships.

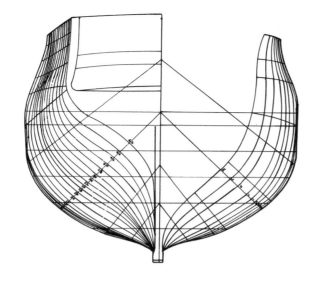

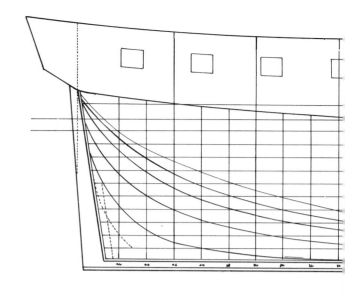

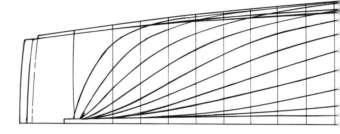

$\mathcal{Y}$oung John Aylwin loved to go with his father, a ship's carpenter, to Hartt Brothers Shipyard on the Boston waterfront. Sometimes he'd sit on the wharf looking out at the forest of masts, ships of every kind and size bobbing and swaying gently at their berths. But this morning he climbed the stairs of a large building to the attic. This was the mold loft. The huge space was empty except for a lone figure, down on his hands and knees, chalking the long, curved lines of a ship's hull on the wooden floor.

It was the biggest ship John had ever seen. His surprise must have been heard. "She is a big one, all right," the kneeling man said as he deftly drew a graceful, sweeping line against a thin wooden ship's curve. "She is a frigate and the largest ship ever built on these shores — 1,576 tons."

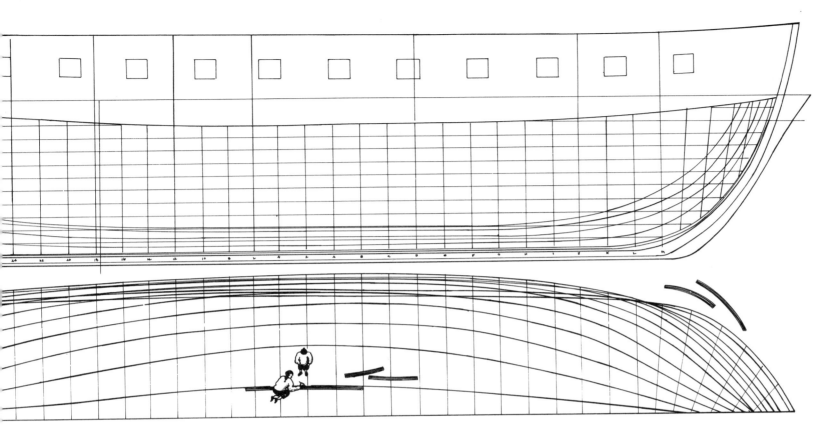

John paced out the length of the frigate. It was almost 200 feet (actually 175 feet) and its beam nearly 50 (45 feet, 2 inches). He had often watched the lines laid down on this floor — brigs, schooners, and barks, all merchantmen — but a man-of-war!

When John remarked on the graceful sheer of the bow and the nicely raked stem and cutwater (the leading edge of the ship), the draftsman stopped midline and for the first time looked up from his work, astonished. "My name is Claghorne, George Claghorne," he said, regarding John with curiosity.

"Did you design her?" John asked.

"No. She is the work of Mr. Joshua Humphreys, at the capital down in Philadelphia," Mr. Claghorne explained. "I am in charge of her construction. She's to be called *Constitution*, the name chosen by President Washington himself." Then he motioned John to follow him over to a workbench at one end of the loft.

Mr. Claghorne showed John a beautiful wooden model. It was a frigate in miniature — well, half a frigate. Since both sides of a ship are the same, symmetrical, it was enough just to model half the hull.

John could not help running his fingers over the polished wood to get the feel of the great ship in his hands, from the rounded bow back along the keel to the tuck of the stern. He rolled and turned the model all around, looked at it from above as a soaring gull might and from below, like a whale. He imagined the bow cutting through the waves and a frothy white wake trailing behind.

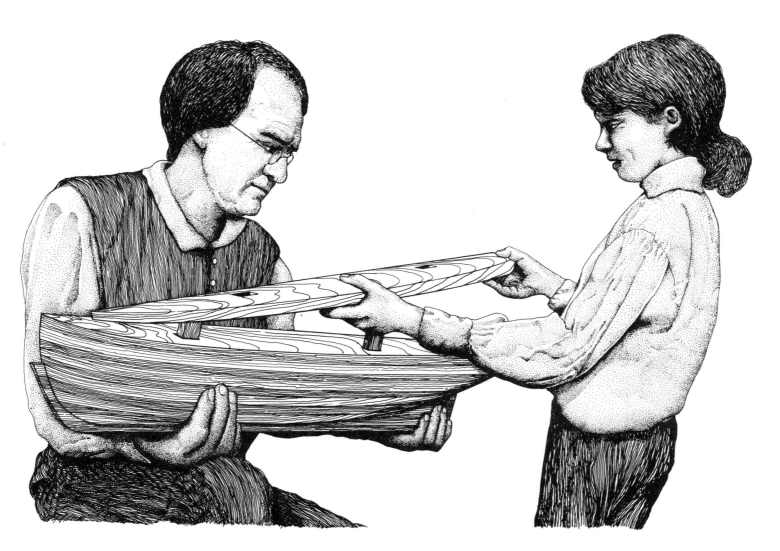

Ship designers of the day first carved the hull in wood. Mr. Humphreys chiseled and whittled and smoothed the wood until his vision of the frigate began taking shape. From time to time he showed the model to other shipbuilders, to sea captains, and to old sailors, who added their years of sailing experience to the final shape of the hull. Some recommended lighter, agile ships with smaller guns, which could chase and overtake pirates in shallow waters. But Mr. Humphreys was not thinking only of pirates. These few expensive ships would be all America would have for some years to come. Someday, he feared, they would have to fight the dreaded men-of-war of the English or French navy.

Mr. Claghorne explained to John how the model had started out as separate planks stacked one on top of the other. After the model was finished, the planks, or "lifts," were taken apart, and each lift was traced out on paper, one on top of the other — "taking off the lines," it was called.

These lines were enlarged to become the full-size ship on the mold loft floor.

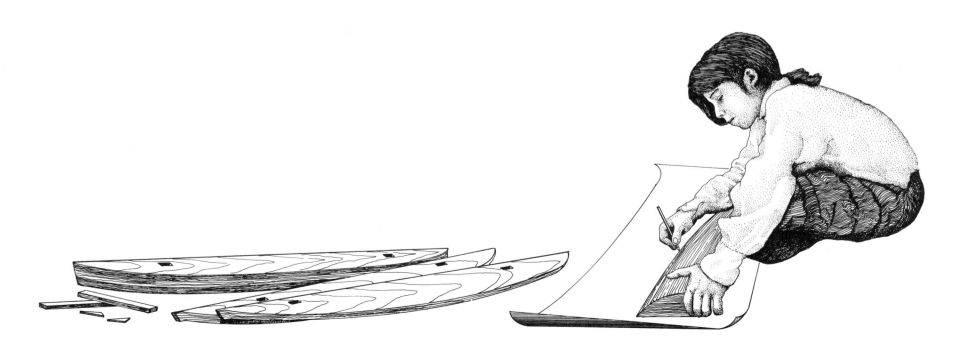

John knew that as the drawings were completed, ship's carpenters would be sent in all directions to select and cut the trees for the frigate's timbers, planking, and decking. With them they carried molds, thin wooden patterns traced right from Mr. Claghorne's lines. These would be held up to tree trunks, limbs, and roots to make sure they were the right shape and size.

Knees — brackets that support the decks — were hewn from the natural curve of the trunk and root. Frame pieces called futtocks and other crooked pieces would be hewn from gently curving limbs and trunks. The V-shaped floor timbers that joined the frames at the keel came from the crotches where two limbs or trunks come together. The planking and decking would be sawn from straight timber — all by hand.

The first task of the woodcutter was to square off all four sides of the timber with a broadaxe. Then he'd lay the mold on the flat face and trace the outline into the wood with a timber scribe. When he had finished hewing out the piece and smoothing it, hardly an adze mark showed.

Humphreys called for the very best woods to make the strongest frigates that had ever sailed the seas. From New Jersey, South Carolina, and Georgia came pitch pine for deck beams, and from Maine, white pine for masts and spars. From Massachusetts came white oak for deck and hull planking. The pines in New England grew to more than 200 feet and could be 3 feet across, so they were perfect for the masts — Humphreys wanted them heavier than was the custom, to hold

more sail and withstand cannon shot. His list of materials also included solid white oak timbers, 18 inches by 24 inches by 100 feet long. Holding it all together would be locust branches fashioned into fifty thousand trunnels, or wooden pegs. In all, some fifteen hundred trees covering sixty acres would be cut for *Constitution*.

Important to Humphreys's plan was the live oak tree. Its wood is harder, stronger, and more durable than any other. A single branch can weigh tons. Shipbuilders figured that live oak, even with constant exposure to salt water, could last forty to fifty years. To harvest the live oak, sixty axmen and thirty ship's carpenters would be sent south, among them John's father.

So it was that early one morning John followed his father to the harbor, this time not just to watch and dream but to board a two-masted schooner, the *Maggie Turner*. He stood on the deck as the hawsers were cast off, the crew all around him tugging mightily on lines. Suddenly the sails set, flapping and billowing, filling with wind. The bowsprit swung out like an arrow pointing toward the opening to the harbor and, beyond, the sea. To the south lay Charleston and Savannah and weeks of live oaking on St. Simons Island, off the coast of Georgia.

John found the hot, humid seacoast unbearable. And soon he was missing his mother's cooking. He was not used to the southern woodcutters' meals of fatty salt meats, hardtack (with or without weevils), and molasses tea "strong enough to float an axe." He prided himself that this was, after all, the way sailors ate at sea. But few New Englanders would work here long, so the woodcutters' first task was to arrange for local woodsmen — Africans brought to the islands as slaves — to cut the trees and hew the ship's timbers.

Hard, hard work. A live oak trunk can be 17 feet thick, its limbs 70 feet long and more. Deciding which trees to fell took a practiced eye. Sizing up his trees, the shipwright relied on all his senses, the color of the bark, and — one of the best signs — the pungent, clean scent of the tannin. He would strike the trunk or a branch with the poll of his axe and listen carefully for the clear sharp *clack* of sound wood.

John would be called on to sharpen axes, help heave a timber, fetch water, gather kindling, tend the cooking fire, or lift the huge iron kettle heavy with potatoes and salt beef. But he spent as much time as he could in the cool under the canopy of a live oak's olive-green leaves trailing feathery Spanish moss. He would doze in the sultry heat, lulled by the rhythmic thudding of axes and adzes. And he would dream of someday sailing before the mast on a sleek, powerful frigate.

14

Soon schooners arrived at Hartt's laden with the *Constitution's* planking, masts, and live oak timbers. Now the work of building could begin.

The shipwrights had all they needed to start — and finish — the new ship. Though her lines were splendid and her size exceptional for a frigate, construction followed centuries of shipbuilding tradition. The proportions for a seaworthy craft were given in tables and charts written many decades before. Most of what was needed was right there in the gnarled, skilled hands of master shipwrights and in the strong backs of eager apprentices.

So the work began of laying down the keel — the backbone of the ship. Then the stem went up at the bow and the sternpost, much as would be done for a schooner, brig, or any other merchantman. But at the next stage, when the frames that make up the ribs of the ship's skeleton were put up, the genius of Mr. Humphreys began to show.

Shipbuilders commonly spaced the frames 2 feet or more apart. But in Humphreys's frigate, less than 2 inches would be left between the massive live oak frames, the spaces packed with crushed rock salt to help preserve the wood. Once planked inside and out, *Constitution's* hull would be a solid wall of wood almost 2 feet thick.

From sunrise to sunset, six days a week, the shipyard sang with the *slip, slip* of planes, the rasp of saws, and hatchets, hammers, broadaxes, mauls, and mallets tapping in a hundred rhythms. Wood chips covered the ground ankle deep and filled the air with incense. John worked every day now, and returned home at dusk tired, itching from sawdust, his hands growing harder and harder with calluses and pitch.

One morning, instead of heading toward the shipyard, John followed familiar winding paths through Boston to the old granary on Park Street, just across from the Common. He climbed its steep stairs to the loft and emerged into an ocean of snowy flax canvas cascading toward him in waves over the floor. In the billowy folds John could see men, some busily sewing and talking, others cutting out shapes on the floor with knives. He had found the right place. These were *Constitution's* sails, and more cloth than he had ever seen before.

More than an acre of cloth. The American frigate, according to Humphreys's plan, would carry more sail than any other ship of her type. In all, she would have more than forty flaxen sails — mainsails and topsails, topgallants and royals, jibs and spankers and staysails. And at the very top would be a skysail.

Making sails is hard work. Since the canvas could be woven only 22 inches wide, many widths had to be pieced and double-stitched together to make a whole sail. This actually made the sail stronger than if it were one piece. The main topsail was more than 80 feet wide at its foot and more than 50 feet high. Every one of the countless stitches was sewn by hand with a triangular-pointed sail needle. This meant forcing the needle through as many as a dozen layers in the corners. The sailmaker wore a sailor's palm, a fingerless leather glove with a metal disk set into the palm which, like a thimble, pushed against the eye of the needle. Close at hand was a grease horn, an ox horn filled with fat, into which the sailmaker dipped his needle to make it pierce the cloth more easily.

After the sails were pieced together, heavy tarred hemp rope was stitched all around to reinforce the edge. Then thousands of eyelets were sewn in, like round buttonholes through which ropes were passed to lash the sails to the spars. Just moving all that canvas around the loft was work enough. The main topsail alone weighed more than half a ton.

The blast of Furnace Hope lights up the Providence, Rhode Island, night sky for miles around. The furnace is kept alive by a village of families: colliers make charcoal and fillers dump it by the barrow load into the 2,500-degree fire, while teamsters bring wagonloads of iron bars called "pigs" and crushed oyster shells to help the iron flow freely. All the time, the waterwheel turns, working the huge leather bellows that blow blasts of air through the hot coals.

Making cannon was heavy industry in those days. In fact, the 24-pounders, weighing almost three tons when they came out of the sand, were the heaviest castings ever poured at an American furnace. Back before the Revolution — barely twenty years earlier — not a single cannon was cast on these shores. But American ironmasters learned how, and Furnace Hope began turning out 18-pounders, the largest naval guns ever cast in the colonies.

At the hearth, the ironmaster looks through a peephole into the furnace's fiery orange heart. He knows by the color if the iron is right.

Out on the floor molders make sand molds from a wooden pattern the exact shape of a cannon. The molds are made in short sections in an iron flask or box: first the sprue and muzzle, then a section of barrel, then another and another, and finally the ornate cascabel, the knob at the back of the gun. When the molds are finished, the wooden patterns are removed and the hollow sand molds are stacked and buried in a deep pit in the floor until only the opening to the muzzle can be seen in the sand. Finally, the keepers lay a line of stone runners, making a channel between the furnace hearth and the opening to the cannon mold.

"Iron's up," the founder shouts to the keepers, and a clanging bell calls the crew to come help. The founder chips away the clay plug in the opening to the hearth.

Suddenly sparks explode out onto the heads and shoulders of the workers, and a bright glow fills the casting shed as a stream of white-hot iron runs out of the hearth, along the stone runners, across the floor, and down into the mold. Deep in the sand, two of *Constitution's* cannon cool slowly from yellow to orange to cherry red to cold gray.

Joshua Humphreys intended *Constitution* to be the most heavily armed frigate on the seas. His plans called for forty-four guns, including the big guns of the day, muzzle-loaded 24-pounders (that's the weight of the iron shot fired). But when she entered service, *Constitution* carried thirty 24-pounders along with sixteen 18-pounders and fourteen 12-pounders — sixty guns in all!

After three days, the solid iron castings are removed from the sand and sent to be

bored out. The work is precise. If the windage — the looseness of the shot in the bore — is too great, the shot will not fly far and true or strike hard. Finally, the castings are proofed by firing heavier powder charges than would normally be used. Back in Boston, carpenters are already at work building the heavy wheeled carriages of elm on which the cannon will be mounted. There they will stand, lined up, awaiting the day when *Constitution* is launched and ready to be fitted out.

As the days and months passed, John watched the frigate take shape. They'd become friends. When he stood barefoot in the sand looking up, he felt at once tiny and graced by her presence. He knew her when she was just rough-hewn timbers piled on a sea island beach — no, before that, when he traced her lines on the mold loft floor. That was almost three years ago. He's grown another foot taller, she more than forty.

It is a rare and wonderful feeling to stand at the keel of a great ship, her hull curving overhead. John took a long last look. Once launched, she would live in the sea. Her bright copper sheets would turn the green of the Atlantic waters, almost invisible under the waves.

Copper sheathing was a recent idea in shipbuilding. Wooden hulls quickly become covered with seaweed and millions of sea creatures. Worms bore into the hull. Barnacles and mussels encrust the planking and reduce the ship's speed. But barnacles don't like copper, so a copper-bottomed ship stays smooth and the planking needs replacing less frequently. There were as yet no copper smelters in America, so the copper sheets were brought from England. John was there the day that over four thousand copper plates were delivered, along with more than four hundred thousand copper nails.

But John had another reason for wanting to be there that day. He heard a familiar voice, and, craning around the end of the keel, he managed to get a glimpse of a short, round figure talking with Mr. Claghorne. Paul Revere had arrived, bringing the copper sheets and nails. Mr. Revere and his metalsmiths had hammered out every one of the nails. They also cast all of the copper and bronze fittings — bolts and spikes, rudder gudgeons and pintles, hammock irons, links, and hundreds of other sturdy pieces, among them the 242-pound ship's bell.

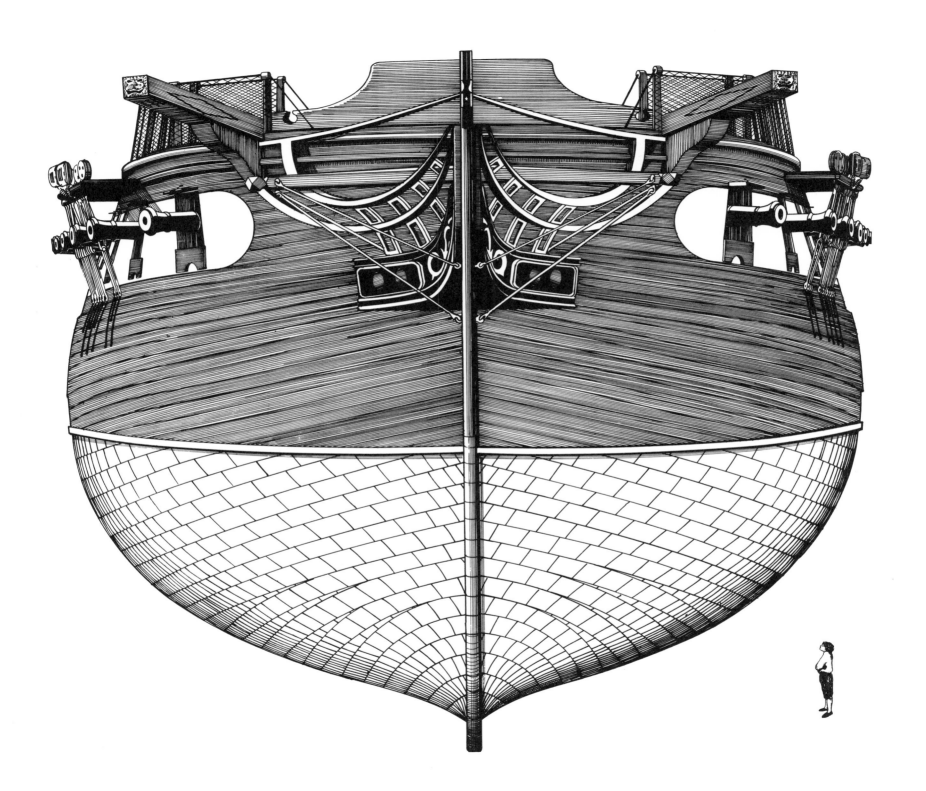

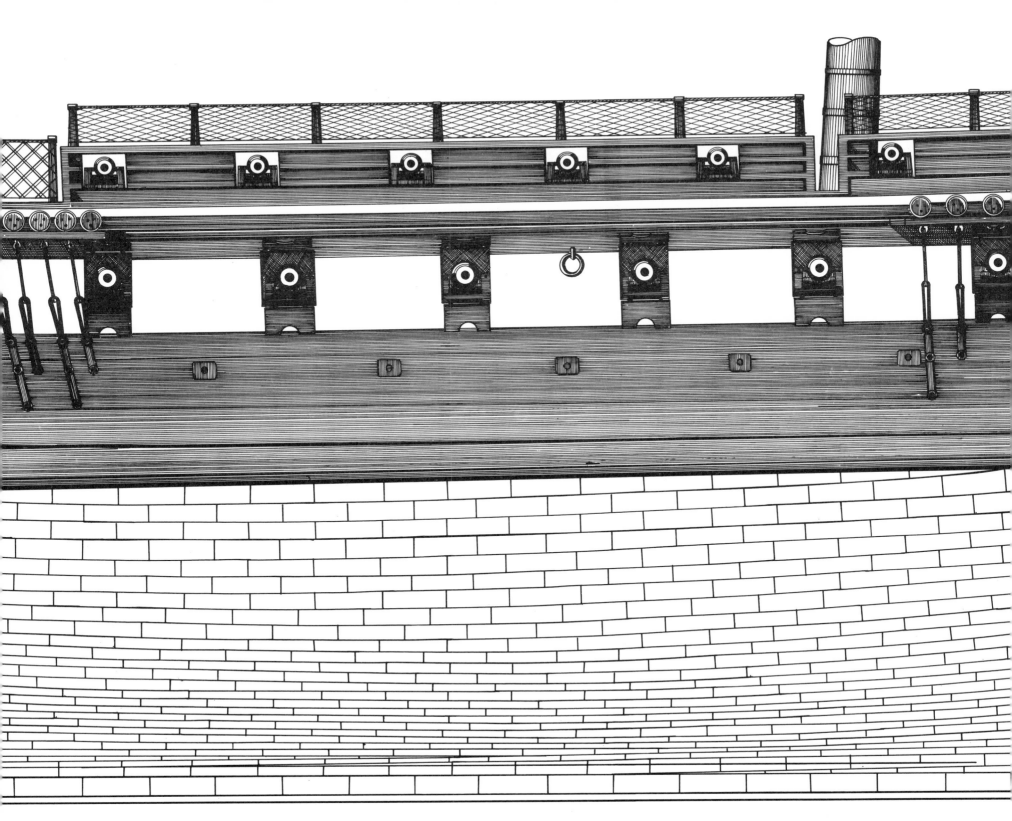

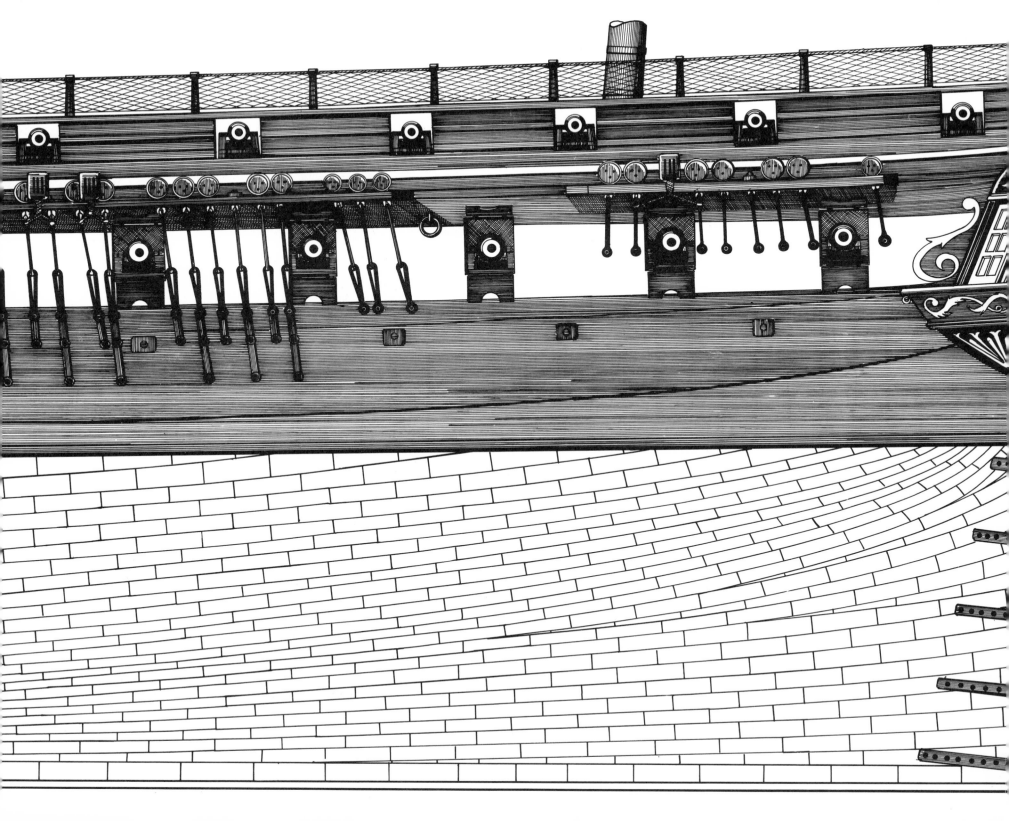

John's hard work on the ship didn't go unnoticed. One day Mr. Claghorne asked the boy he had met three years before in the dusty mold loft if he would like to be one of his assistants. Now they would spend more time together, and Mr. Claghorne would teach John all he knew about building ships.

"Mr. Humpreys faced some difficult decisions," he explained to John one day as they stood looking up at the nearly completed ship. "He knew these few ships were going to be almost the entire American navy. Six frigates. Why, the English have more than a thousand fighting ships — just try to imagine that many ships, John — many of them first-rate line-of-battle ships with three or four gun decks, thirty-inch-thick hulls, and a hundred guns or more!

"Well, Mr. Humphreys decided on frigates. But these are not ordinary frigates, mind you, like the English and French build. *Constitution* will be large enough to stay at sea for months and go anywhere in the world she is needed. She will be fast enough to outrun a first-rate ship. But believe me, John, she will master every ship of her rating she meets. And with her fast lines and spread of canvas, why, she can outsail anything in her class."

When John asked why a builder couldn't just add a few more guns or have all 24-pounders rather than the smaller 18-pounders, Mr. Claghorne explained the problem. "Shipbuilders must always make compromises. Think of it this way. Each 24-pounder adds about three tons. More cannon means heavier timbers and planking supporting the gun deck. Since each cannon needs a crew of twelve men — oh, and a boy; let us not forget the powder monkey — each gun adds to the crew and ship's stores. And then there's the weight of the shot. Our frigate will sail with about five thousand round shot, five hundred double-headed shot, and five hundred grape and canister shot. Add to that two hundred barrels of gunpowder — about ten tons — and she is getting heavier and heavier, and slower.

"Find a balance. That's what you do building ships, John. In his design, Mr. Humphreys found a deadly balance of speed and cannon power."

A few days later, on October 21, 1797, John watched *Constitution* come alive as she slid down the ways and into the water with a tremendous splash.

Epilogue

"Clear ship for action," Captain Isaac Hull ordered. The drums beat "to quarters," and four hundred men moved smartly into position around *Constitution's* guns. "All eyes were turned in the direction of the strange sail," recalled gunner Moses Smith, "and quick as thought studding-sails were out, fore and aft. The noble frigate fairly bounded over the billows."

It was 1812 and Joshua Humphreys's fears had come to be reality: the United States and England were again at war. For years, English captains had felt it was their right to stop and board American ships and impress crew members whom they claimed to be deserters. Then it happened. A British ship, HMS *Leopard*, actually fired on an American frigate, the USS *Chesapeake*, just off Norfolk, Virginia. With *Chesapeake's* guns still secured for sea, Captain James Barron had no choice but to strike his colors. British officers boarded and took four sailors with them, leaving behind in the splintered wreckage twenty-two Americans dead or wounded.

By this time, one thousand American ships had been taken prize by the English and the French. Over six thousand Americans had been impressed into His Britannic Majesty's Navy. The English, Thomas Jefferson wrote, "have touched a chord which vibrates in every heart. Now then is the time to settle the old and the new." President Madison called for war.

All was ready. Hammocks had been stowed in netting to protect the crew from flying splinters. Tubs of water were put out for sponging guns, slaking the thirst of gunners, and dousing fires. The tompions had been removed from the mouths of the cannon. Gun decks were sanded lest they become slippery with blood. Barefoot powder monkeys raced belowdecks to the magazine and returned with the first charges. When they swung open the gun port shutters, the crew looked out on a British frigate, HMS *Guerriere*, with forty-nine guns, Captain James Dacres commanding.

"Cast loose the battery," Captain Hull ordered. Less than five minutes had

passed since the call to quarters. The guns were run out and, with a practiced precision, loaded — cartridge, shot, and wad. The crews stood tense, quiet.

Guerriere's batteries began long-distance firing, the usual opening of a naval battle. The object was to damage the enemy's rigging and ability to maneuver. A shot crashed into *Constitution's* foremast. Another splintered the decking. Captain Hull moved confidently among the crew. "Men, now do your duty. Your officers cannot have entire command over you now. Each man must do all in his power for his country."

The crew was impatient to fire, the tension in the air almost unbearable. But

Hull stood watching, waiting. Then he called out for all to hear: "Sailing master! Lay her alongside!"

Constitution's black hull heeled to the pressure of the wind in her sails, the Stars and Stripes streaming from her mizzen peak. The wind drove the great frigate closer and closer to the Britisher, until the two ships lay but a pistol-shot apart. At last came the captain's command to fire: "Now boys, hull her!" The gun captains stood at the ready, firing lanyards in their hands. Steady. Here comes the roll, to the top of the wave, beginning to roll downward — FIRE! As one, the lanyards were pulled, flintlocks snapped down, and a broadside of 24-pound shot smashed into *Guerriere's* hull.

The crews moved quickly to their guns as the captains called out in cadence: Stop vent! Sponge! Load! Run out your guns! Another broadside, and another. American gunners were trained to fire on the downward roll so that their shot hulled the enemy below the waterline. The crews worked at their peak now, firing a round every minute and a half.

Guerriere's gunners watched in horror as their shot, fired point-blank, simply bounced off *Constitution's* hull. The story is told that one British sailor cried out in desperation, "Look, her sides are made of iron."

Twenty minutes later *Guerriere's* mizzenmast was in the water. Captain Hull ordered the guns loaded with grapeshot. Then, just as the sailing master brought *Constitution* across the enemy's bow, the gunners loosed a terrible hail of iron, raking the length of *Guerriere's* decks. The ships were so close at times that twice their rigging fouled. Broadside after broadside smashed and splintered the Britisher — in all, 953 rounds — until her fore and mainmasts were also down and she was taking on water fast. Finally, Captain Dacres, wounded, fired a gun to leeward, away from the action, in token of surrender.

Remembering the dead and dying on *Chesapeake's* decks, *Constitution's* crew, to a man, gave their captain three hearty cheers. Captain Hull passed among his men. Stopping at the wheel, he clasped the shoulders of the young sailing master, shaking him heartily. " 'Tis a good day's work, Mister Aylwin."

Acknowledgments

A book, no less than a great ship, requires the skills of many, each of whom brings to the task special talents and knowledge. Margherita Desy and Ann Grimes welcomed me to the USS Constitution Museum and the treasures of their library and then took a continuing interest in the book's progress. Patrick Otton and Don Turner took me through *Constitution* in dry dock and the restoration shops. Over the months, Patrick was always there to answer a landlubber's endless questions and to come up with exactly the drawings, views, and details I needed.

Much of the work was done by phone, a continent away. Judy Lund of the Old Dartmouth Historical Society sent me photographs from the collection and introduced me to Gary Adair of Mystic Seaport, who told me about sailmaking. From Kathy Flynn came photographs of the model of *Constitution* in the collection of the Peabody Essex Museum, and from old friend Betsy Woodman, stories of Newburyport's own *Polly*. Questions about casting cannon brought answers and envelopes full of stuff from Steven Lubar, Donald Pierce, Ed Olmstead, and the old ironmaster himself, Ed Rutsch.

Ty Martin introduced me to the genius of Joshua Humphreys and the fine points of *Constitution's* construction. He and Leon Kaufman gave the manuscript careful readings and added many authentic touches.

I would also like to thank Bill and Ethie Bass for graciously allowing me to use their beautiful conjectural reconstructions of *Constitution's* early phases, upon which I based my drawings. And, finally, a special thanks to Howard Harris, Malcolm Lane, and Paul Brower; to my editor, Audrey Bryant, who magically showed up in the right place at just the right time; and to Pat Malone, whose wise counsel helped me to get down to work and lay the keel.

Manufactured in the United States of America

HOR 10 9 8 7 6 5 4 3 2 1

Library of Congress Cataloging-in-Publication Data
Old Ironsides / written and illustrated by David Weitzman.
    p. cm.
Summary: A fictionalized account of the design and construction of the U.S.S. Constitution, told through the eyes of a boy whose father is one of the ship's carpenters.
ISBN 0-395-74678-7
1. Constitution (Frigate)—Juvenile fiction. [1. Constitution (Frigate) — Fiction.]
I. Title.
PZ7.W44818401   1996
[Fic] — dc20
95-52485
CIP   AC

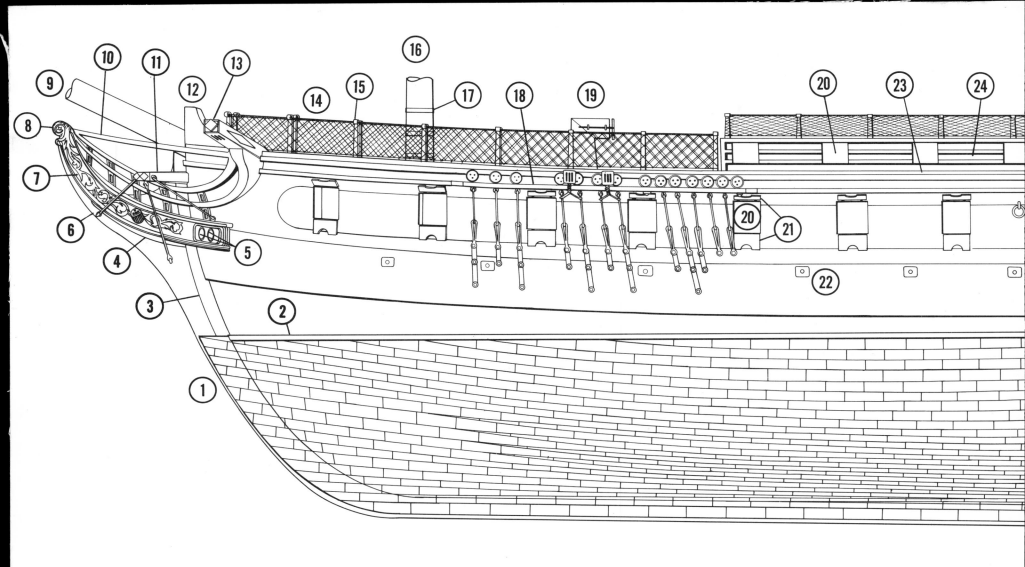

Air ports (22)

Apron (3)

Base rail (46)

Billethead (8)

Bow head rails (10)

Bowsprit (9)

Bowsprit pinrail (12)

Bulwark (24)

Cathead (13)

Chain plates (29)

Channel wale (36)

Charlie Noble (19)

Cheek knees or bolster (4)

Copper sheathing (56)

Cutwater or forefoot (1)

Deadeyes (31)

Dressing belt (35)

Drumhead lacing (42)

Foremast (16)

Fore studding sail boom (18)

Foretack boomkin (11)

Gallery counter (44)

Gangway (26)

Gudgeons (53)

Gun ports (20)

Gun port shutters (21)

Halyard blocks (32)

Hammock netting (14)

Hammock netting irons (15)

Hawsepipes (5)